For Jameson,
who's watched the Ooga
video a thousand times
and still loves it.

Alan St. Jean

Published by Oren Village, LLC, Sunbury, Ohio.
For information or permission to reproduce, please contact
alanstjean@gmail.com or write to Alan St. Jean, PO Box 900, Sunbury, Ohio 43074.
Text set in Anime Ace 2.0.
Cover design by Lilla Hangay. Illustrations were digitally rendered.

Names:
St. Jean, Alan, author.
Title:
Ooga Looga / by Alan St. Jean.
Description:
First edition. | Sunbury, Ohio: Oren Village, LLC, [2020] | Series: The young authors collection ; v. 1. |
Audience: children. | Summary: It is the age of cave men. And dinosaurs! Ooga Looga was out hunting
one day with his pet turtle, Dave, when the tables were turned. The hunter became the hunted!
Join us on our dangerous journey where we learn Ooga Looga's fate...--Publisher.
Identifiers:
ISBN: 978-1-7333020-0-5
Subjects:
LCSH: Children, Prehistoric--Juvenile fiction. | Dinosaurs--Juvenile fiction. | Turtles--Juvenile fiction. |
Hunting stories. | Children's stories. | CYAC: Prehistoric peoples--Fiction. | Dinosaurs--Fiction. |
Turtles--Fiction. | Hunting--Fiction. | LCGFT: Hunting fiction. | Picture books.
Classification:
LCC: PZ7.S14245 O64 2020 | DDC: [Fic]--dc23

Ooga Looga

by Alan St. Jean

The Young Authors Collection • Volume 1

IT'S BEEN A LONG TIME SINCE THE AGE OF THE DINOSAURS, ONE OF A KIND HE LIVED WAY UP HIGH ON A MOUNTAIN THAT TOUCHED THE EDGE OF THE SKY...

HIS NAME WAS OOGA LOOGA.

HE LIVED IN A CAVE WITH A TURTLE NAMED DAVE

DAVE

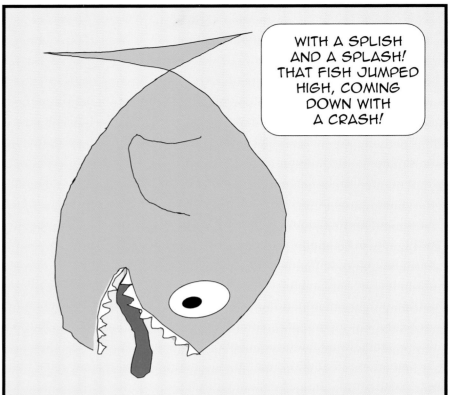

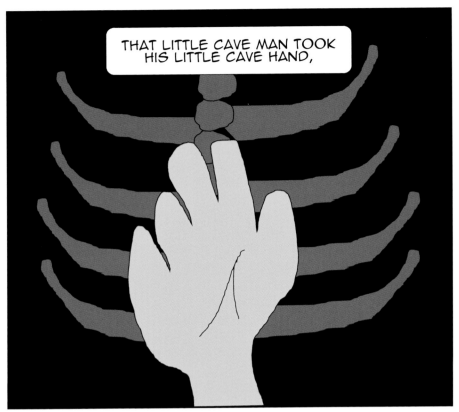

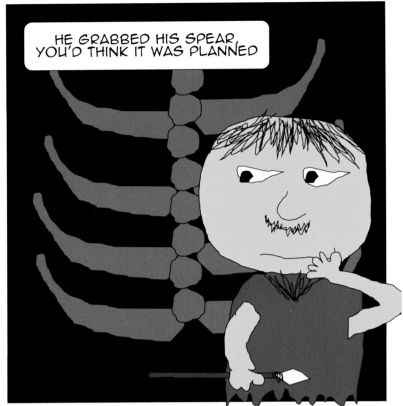

HE DRUG THAT FISHY ALL LUMPY AND SQUISHY
UP TO HIS CAVE, WITH JUST ONE WISHY,
TO COOK THAT BEAST AND FILL A BIG DISHY –
AND FEED OOGA LOOGA!

THEN THE T-REX REACHED HIS FEROCIOUS ARM INSIDE THE CAVE, BUT IT WAS NOT ALARMING.
HA! TINY ARMS ARE KIND OF CHARMING!
MOM

THE CAVEMAN PAUSED
AS HE STARED AT THE CLAWS
OF THE GIANT BEAST WITH THE GIANT JAWS.

THE THOUGHT OF BABIES
MADE HIM PAUSE
...'CAUSE...

BABIES LOVE
OOGA LOOGA!

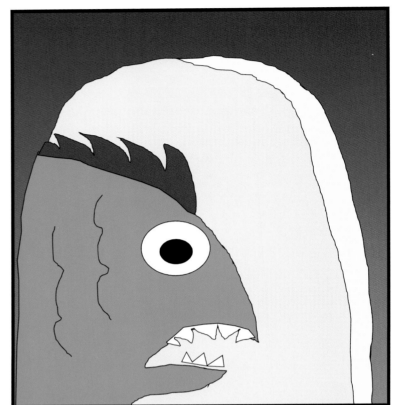

HE TUGGED IT IN THE MONSTER'S GREAT BIG MOUTH,
WITH RAZOR SHARP TEETH HANGIN' ALL ABOUT
AND THEN WITH A CHOMP, THE T-REX CLOSED HIS SNOUT...POOR OOGA LOOGA!

THE T-REX BRAYED AS HE WALKED AWAY
A FRESH HOT MEAL WAS A PRETTY GOOD DAY.

WHEN HE SUDDENLY STOPPED
AND STARTED TO SWAY.

THEN A CHUBBY, DIRTY AND WEATHERED HAND

CUT A REALLY BIG HOLE IN THE TUMMY GLAND.

AND WHO POPPED OUT? OUR FAVORITE CAVE MAN! IT'S OOGA LOOGA!

HELPFUL HINTS
(DON'T WORRY, OOGA AND HIS FRIENDS WILL HELP AS YOU GO.)

WHEN YOU WRITE:
ADD DETAILS, LIKE:
WHAT IS YOUR CHARACTER DOING?
WHY ARE THEY DOING IT?
HOW ARE THEY FEELING?

WHEN YOU DRAW:
*DRAW YOUR PICTURE WITH A PENCIL FIRST
SO YOU CAN MAKE CHANGES EASILY.
*THEN, COLOR IT!
(THAT'S HOW ILLUSTRATORS DO IT)
*ALSO, ADD DETAILS! SHOW THE
SURROUNDINGS. BE CREATIVE!

ARE YOU READY TO START??

LET'S MEET YOUR CHARACTER

IN THIS SCENE, DRAW A NICE, BIG PICTURE OF YOUR CHARACTER. BE SURE TO USE A LOT OF DETAIL BECAUSE WE'RE INTRODUCING THEM TO THE READER. THIS IS THEIR PHYSICAL APPEARANCE.

IN THE BUBBLE BOX, TELL US TWO THINGS ABOUT YOUR CHARACTER. ARE THEY GOOD, OR BAD? ARE THEY HAPPY, OR SAD? ARE THEY SILLY, OR ARE THEY SNEAKY? THINGS LIKE THAT. THIS HELPS US INDERSTAND YOUR CHARACTER'S PERSONALITY.

Thing one:

Thing two:

LET'S START THE STORY: BEGINNING

USE THE BUBBLE BOX TO WRITE THE BEGINNING OF YOUR STORY, THEN DRAW A PICTURE TO BRING YOUR WORDS TO LIFE. MAKE SURE YOU DRAW THEIR SURROUNDINGS, TOO. FOR EXAMPLE, IF THEY'RE IN A JUNGLE, DRAW TREES AND JUNGLE STUFF. IT'S CALLED THE SETTING. DETAILS ARE WHAT MAKE PICTURES AWESOME! DON'T TRY TO DRAW LIKE ANYONE ELSE, JUST DRAW THE WAY YOU DRAW, IT'S YOUR STYLE AND IT IS GOOD ENOUGH! YOU'RE AN ILLUSTRATOR!

One day,

PLOT: THE BIG 'WHY'

WHAT HAPPENS NEXT IN YOUR STORY? DRAW THE SCENE HERE. IN THE BUBBLE BOX, EXPLAIN WHAT IS HAPPENING AND TELL US WHY THE CHARACTER IS DOING WHAT THEY ARE DOING.

Then,

CONFLICT: SOMETHING GOES WRONG

THINGS ARE ABOUT TO GET BAD. CONFLICT HELPS MAKE A STORY MORE INTERESTING.
BASED ON WHAT'S HAPPENING IN THE STORY, TELL US WITH A PICTURE AND WITH YOUR WORDS WHAT HAS
GONE WRONG FOR YOUR CHARACTER. ALSO, TELL US HOW THE CHARACTER FEELS ABOUT THE CONFLICT.

Suddenly,

MORE CONFLICT!

OH, NO! AS IF THINGS WEREN'T BAD ENOUGH, SOMETHING ELSE WENT WRONG! THIS IS AWFUL!
WAIT A MINUTE. HMMM. NO, THIS IS FUN!

Things got worse because

RESOLUTION

CONFLICT IS FUN IN A STORY, BUT WE NEED TO FIX THE PROBLEM SO THAT THE READER FEELS SATISFIED AT THE END. IF WE DON'T FIX THE PROBLEM, THE STORY IS NO FUN TO READ.
DRAW A PICTURE AND USE YOUR WORDS TO TELL US WHAT HAPPENS NEXT THAT CAN FIX THE PROBLEMS FOR YOUR CHARACTER. DO THEY FIGURE OUT A WAY TO FIX THEIR OWN PROBLEM?
OR, DID SOMEONE ELSE SAVE THEM?

The day was saved when

ENDING

WE'RE NOT SIMPLY GOING TO SAY 'THE END' HERE...THAT'S SILLY AND MAKES THE STORY WAY TOO SHORT. LET'S HAVE FUN WITH THIS. IN THE BUBBLE BOX, TELL US WHAT YOUR CHARACTER LEARNED FROM THEIR EXPERIENCE. THEN, DRAW A PICTURE THAT SHOWS WHAT BECAME OF THEM IN THE FUTURE! DID THEY BECOME FAMOUS? DID THEY GET MARRIED? I KNOW...EWWW!

Our character learned